# HISTORY MYSTERY

PAY ATTENTION, PUPILS-- TIME FOR YOUR HISTORY LESSON.

WE'RE ALL EARS!

..BLAH! BLAH! ...AND QUEEN ELIZABETH WAS A VERY BEAUTIFUL QUEEN ...

COO!

BLAH FA...

SIGH!

SWORDSMEN, EH? ...

DAY-DREAMING

...BET THERE WERE LOTS OF DUELS!

WAHEY! DEFEND YOURSELF, KNAVE!

EH?

Several whacks later—

RIGHT! NO MORE DREAMING—YOUR HEADS ARE FULL OF NONSENSE!

Teacher continues—

DRONE! DRONE! BLAH-BLAH! DRONE! ...

Soon—

HMMM!

YOU'RE NOT LISTENING, ARE YOU, SOLID PUPIL?

HUH?

JAB

...BLAH! BLAH! ...

GROAN! THIS IS THE LONGEST BEFORE - DINNER SPEECH I'VE EVER HEARD—WE'VE BEEN LISTENING TO HIM FOR SIX NIGHTS!

STARVING

THAT DOES IT—NO MORE HISTORY! GET OUT YOUR MATHS BOOKS!

SLAM!

YOU'RE NOT LISTENING!

SWISH!

POP! POP! POP! POP!

...DURING THE FRENCH REVOLUTION, FRANCE WAS FULL OF COLOURFUL SWORDSMEN...

WOW!

HAVE AT U, VARLET!

ERK!

JAB

BOO! DOWN WITH THE EVIL TYRANT!

But Plug wakes up—

ULP! WHAT HAVE I DONE?

SNORT! I'LL SOON PUT AN END TO THIS REVOLUTION!

BUT, OF COURSE, MON GENERAL!

SMIFFY'S BEST NAPOLEON IMPRESSION

—AND TEACHER WAS TALKING ABOUT THE AMERICAN CIVIL WAR!

OH, GO BACK TO SLEEP, IDIOTIC IDIOT! AHA! THE DUKE OF WELLINGTON BEATS NAPOLEON ONCE AGAIN!

TEACHER'S WELLY

MUMMFF!

NOW WE COME TO KING ARTHUR AND THE KNIGHTS OF THE ROUND TABLE...

HISTORY

OH, PLEASE CARRY ON! WE LOVE HISTORY!

MOVED

YOU'D NEVER BELIEVE THEY LIKED HISTORY IF YOU SAW THESE...

EXAM PAPER

WHICH ELIZABETHAN QUEEN RULED ENGLAND IN THE ELIZABETHAN PERIOD?
----King Kong----

WHAT WAS FRANCIS DRAKES FIRST NAME?
----Pass----

NAME 3 KNIGHTS OF THE ROUND TABLE.
Monday, Tuesday and Bathnight

WHO WON AT HASTINGS IN 1066?
Mancester United 4-2 after extra time.

0/100    0/100    0/100

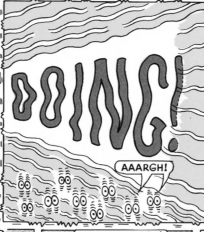

# WHEN I GROW UP

*I'D LIKE TO BE A FAMOUS FOOTBALL PLAYER . . .*

FIRST IN ATTACK, THEN IN DEFENCE —
I'D POP UP EVERYWHERE.

HUH!

WELL SAVED, SIDNEY!

NO-ONE COULD TAKE THE BALL FROM ME—
I'D PLAY WITH STYLE AND GRACE.

KICK

I'M PRETTY BRILLIANT
EVEN NOW . . .

KICK

SPLUTCH!

THUNK!

. . . AT FALLING ON MY FACE!

# BASH STREET Sporting Records

FATTY WAS OUR TOP BATSMAN AT CRICKET — 1,000 RUNS NOT OUT . . .

HOI, UMPIRE! I CAN'T SEE THE STUMPS!

STUMPS

. . . ONLY TEA AND CAKES GOT HIM OUT!

CRACK!

HOWZAT?

SLURP!

OUR FOOTBALL TEAM HAD A WALKOVER VICTORY . . .

KICK

. . . AFTER THE OPPOSITION'S BOOTS WERE — ER — "LOST" JUST BEFORE THE MATCH.

AT TENNIS WE HAD A SECRET WEAPON . . .

ZONK!

WAP!

. . . PLUG'S EARS!

ZONK!

WAP!

WAP!

THANKS TO THEIR SPECIAL BATON, OUR RELAY TEAM WON EVERY RACE.

OVER TO YOU, TOOTS!

OLIVE'S SPRINGY JELLY HELPED BASH STREET HIGH JUMPERS WIN THE POLE-VAULT — WITHOUT EVEN NEEDING A POLE!

PYOING!

WOW!

OLIVE'S JELLY

PASTE

HEATED ARGUMENT

JANITOR

HERE THEY COME—HORRIBLE LITTLE MONSTERS—MOANED ABOUT THE HEATING LAST WEEK—NEVER HAPPY—GRUMBLE! GRUMBLE!

WHAT DO YOU PESTS WANT?

JANITOR'S ROOM

CANDLE FOR CAKE

HAPPY BIRTHDAY TO YOU...

Soon—

SNARL! I'LL SHOW THE LITTLE HORRORS!

BOILER ROOM

I'LL GIVE THEM A HOT TIME OF IT!

HEAT!

PHEW!

In class—

WHEW! IT'S GETTING RATHER HOT IN HERE!

BATTERY OPERATED FAN

WILT

I'M A COOL CUSTOMER!

'ERBERT'S GLASSES HAVE STEAMED UP

WHERE AM I?

VERY DAFT

I'D BETTER PUT ON EXTRA CLOTHES TO STAY COOL!

LET ME COOL YOU DOWN! HAR—HAR!

SWOOSH!

Later—

IT'S HIGH TIME A TRUCE WAS DECLARED BETWEEN YOURSELVES AND THE JANITOR. MAKE HIM A PEACE OFFERING.

HARUMPH! OH, ALL RIGHT!

And so—

I'M NOT FALLING FOR THAT TRICK AGAIN!

BUT IT'S A REAL PEACE OFFERING!

PROD

SNORT! WAIT TILL I GET MY HANDS ON YOU, YOU VAGABONDS!

HEAD'S STUDY

Then—

I SAY, JANITOR—RATHER HOT TODAY—COULDN'T YOU DAMP DOWN THE JOLLY OLD BOILER, OLD CHAP?

THE BOILER! EEK! I'D FORGOTTEN ALL ABOUT IT!

FOOTBALL CRAZY

STAMPING OUT TROUBLE

CAN ANY PUPIL TELL ME WHAT PHILATELY IS?

PHIL ATELY IS A BOY IN CLASS 4A!

IF FATTY WAS ON TV, H FAT FORM WOULD FILL TELLY SCREEN! HA-H

NASTY, HORRID, FRIGHTFUL, BEASTLY ROTTERS!

SILENCE, CUTHBERT! "PHILATELY" WILL GET YOU NOWHERE!

GLUMPH!

TRADING STAMPS

THE PENNY BLACK IS A RARE AND VALUABLE STAMP.

YOU IGNORANT LOT SHOULD GET A STAMP ALBUM.

WE ALREADY HAVE A STAMP ALBUM!

A POP ALBUM! WHY ARE THE GROUP CALLED "THE STAMPS"?

THE STAMPS ALBUM OF POP HITS

BECAUSE THEIR MUSIC MAKES YOU WANT TO STAMP YOUR FEET!

CEASE THIS DREADFUL RACKET!

STAMP! STAMP! STAMP! STAMP!

TEACHER! TEACHER! THOSE RUFFIANS ARE GOING TO POST YOUR CANE!

WH-WHAT?

EVERYTHING STOPS FOR TEA

TEA BICCIES

GRR! IT'S TIME FOR ME TO STAMP MY AUTHORITY ON THE PESTS!

EVERYTHING STOPS FOR TEA

TEA BICCIES

BUTTERFLY COLLECTI NOW, TEACHER?

CHOMP! GUZZLE! CHEEK!

BULL'S EYES

[JE]LLY [BA]BIES

ALL NONSENSE! PHILATELY IS STAMP COLLECTING. I COLLECT STAMPS.

YOU DO, DO YOU?

CUTHBERT CRINGEWORTHY— TEACHER'S PET.

HOW ABOUT RUBBER STAMPS?

TELL-TALE

CREEP

SNEAK

SWOT

TOADY

LOOK WHAT I HAVE, SIR.

A PENNY BLACK!

GIVE ME STRENGTH!

NO—IT'S A HALF-PENNY STAMP THAT FELL IN THE INKWELL!

TEE-HEE-HEE!

—the playground—

CAN WE BORROW SOME OF YOUR SPARE STAMPS, CUTHBERT?

SO! TAKING AN INTEREST IN A WORTHWHILE HOBBY FOR ONCE!

SPARE STAMPS

STAMP ALBUM

WHAT ARE THEY UP TO WITH TEACHER'S CANE?

LICK THEM AND STICK THEM! SLOOP!

WE'LL GET RID OF THIS FOR GOOD!

TO OUTER MONGOLIA

OH, HORRORS!

NO— SCAMP COLLECTING!

TO OUTER MONGOLIA

AW, BOO!

THWACK!

WHACK!

NOW THE SCAMPS ARE GETTING A LICKING!

# WHEN I GROW UP

*I'D LIKE TO BE A LION STRONG AND FIERCE . . .*

ROAR!

AND IF THE KIDS SHOULD PESTER ME, THEIR TROUSERS I WOULD PIERCE.

OW!

BITE

HOWL!

I'D MAKE THEM BRING ME LOTS OF MILK AND POUR IT IN A DISH.

MOO!

MILK

MILK

POUR

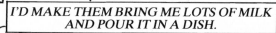

AND THEN I'D SEND THEM OFF TO CATCH A REALLY MONSTER FISH.

DRAG

SALAD CREAM

GASP!

YOUR TIME'S UP

WHERE ARE THOSE PUPILS OF MINE?

TSK! TSK! SHOCKING TARDINESS! I'M IN CLASS BY HALF-PAST SEVEN EVERY MORNING!

DRUM! DRUM!

That instant—

'MORNING, TEACHER!

Later—

I HAVE NEW GLASSES FOR YOU, DIM-SIGHTED ONE.

WHO SAID THAT?

NOW YOU'LL BE ABLE TO SEE TIME PASSING BEFORE YOUR EYES!

Outside—

I HAVE A NEW CARTIE FOR YOU, BOYS.

HOW KIND!

MAY I PRESENT YOU WITH THIS SPECIAL ALARM-CLOCK, DANNY?

DOESN'T LOOK VERY SPECIAL TO ME!

The alarm goes off—

I KNEW THAT WOULD ALARM YOU!

SOAP AND WATER

SOAP AND WATER

SHRIEK!

NICE EAR-RINGS, EH?

SPEAK TO TEACHER!

TEACHER HASN'T SEEN ME!

TUG

AT THE THIRD STROKE IT WILL BE EIGHT O'CLOCK PRECISELY— PIP! PIP! PIP!

POSHEST VOICE

FUNNY—I THOUGHT IT WAS MUCH LATER!

An hour later—

HOW DARE YOU TU UP AT THIS HOUR RAGE! SCOLD!

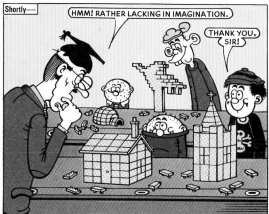

E INVENTED THE OMENS' ROYAL AVAL SERVICE!

HE WAS THE FIRST MAN TO FLY!

RUBBISH! TELL THEM, CUTHBERT!

SIR CHRISTOPHER WREN DESIGNED FAMOUS BUILDINGS. HE WAS A SEVENTEENTH CENTURY ARCHITECT.

A GOLD STAR FOR CLEVERNESS! YOU DUNCES SHOULD TRY TO BE MORE LIKE MY PRIZE PUPIL, CUTHBERT.

MUTTER! HE'S ALWAYS SHOWING US UP!

I, WONDERFUL PUPIL OY OF MY TEACHING CAREER!

MUTTER! SHOWING US UP AGAIN!

CAN ANY PUPIL NAME THE MOST FAMOUS PIECE OF ARCHITECTURE IN THIS DISTRICT?

I'LL MAKE SURE CUTHBERT DOESN'T RAISE HIS HAND THIS TIME!

TONI'S FISH AND CHIP BAR!

I KNOW—YURK!—MY HANDS!

TIED

PLEASE, SIR—IT'S THE ANCIENT BEANOTOWN TOWER.

BAH! THAT SWOT'S DONE IT AGAIN!

... THE DOOR IS MADE OF OAK FROM THE BEANOTOWN FOREST. THE CARPENTER WAS FRED PLANK WHO HAD A WART ON HIS LEFT KNEE...

THBERT LIKES TO MAKE PEOPLE FEEL SMALL!

ANCIENT BEANOTOWN TOWER

THE TOWER WAS BUILT IN 1752...

EXCUSE ME, BUT YOU'RE WRONG AGAIN...

... THE TOWER WAS FINISHED ON MAY 21ST, 1751 AT 10.15 A.M. AND IS MADE UP OF 193,881 BRICKS...

BLUBBER!

I'M AFRAID CUTHBERT'S RIGHT AGAIN, MR GUIDE!

OH, YES YOU WILL! CUTHBERT WILL BE OUR GUIDE!

OH, GOODY!

... AND IN JUNE OF 1751, THE THIRD MAYOR OF BEANOTOWN... DRONE!.. WAFFLE!... COME ALONG, CLASS...

OH, NO! CUTHBERT'S SHOWING US UP AGAIN—UP THE STAIRS, THAT IS!

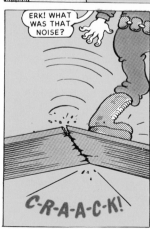

DUE TO TORRENTIAL RAINSTORMS, ALL OF BRITAIN'S SPORT, INCLUDING SWIMMING, HAS BEEN RAINED OFF. WE NOW TAKE YOU OVER TO THE ONLY DRY SPOT IN THE COUNTRY—BASH STREET, WHERE THE SCHOOL IS HOLDING A SPORTS TRIAL...

SEEN AT SPORT

YOUR TURN AT THE HIGH JUMP, PLUG!

Time for an advert—

WARM THEM UP WITH HINE'S SOUP!

ERK!

WHO'LL TRY THROWING THE HAMMER?

NOT THAT SORT OF HAMMER, SMIFFY!

—AND TEACHER THINKS I'M DIM! MY HAMMER WOULD BE EASIER TO THROW! HIS DOESN'T EVEN LOOK LIKE A HAMMER!

—AND WE REJOIN THE BASH STREET SPORTS TRIAL, VIEWERS, JUST IN TIME TO SEE THE HURDLES EVENT.

W-H-I-R-R

THE WINNER!

AHEM!

Weather report—

MORE NEWS ABOUT THE BAD WEATHER, FOLKS—WE'RE IN FOR A DREADFUL SPELL OF RAIN... R-A-N-E.

AND THAT'S THE WORST "SPELL" OF RAIN I'VE HEARD!

Commercial break—

ALWAYS EAT HALF A STRONGARM CHOC BAR...

EYEUCH!

...IT GIVES YOU STRENGTH TO THROW THE OTHER HALF AWAY!

OOYAH!

HELP!

THAT DOES IT! I'M "TYRED" OF ALL THIS!

BITE

NOT LIKE THAT, SILLY BOY!

HOW ABOUT THIS?

GRIPPING WITH SPIKES

GRR! HE'S SHOWING OFF FOR THE TV VIEWERS!

BACK IN A SECOND, VIEWERS, AFTER THE ADVERTS!

STILL, HE'S IN CHARGE, SO HERE GOES!

WAA!

START OF 3-LEGGED RACE

BANG

OOOOOOH! MY TOOTSIES!

DANNY, IT'S A THREE-LEGGED RACE, NOT ONE-LEGGED!

A news flash—

JUST RECEIVED THE LATEST EUROPEAN RESULT— ROMANS 4, GREEKS 0. AND THAT IS A LATE RESULT!

SEEN AT SPORT

— AND NOW THE OBSTACLE RACE!

I'M STUCK!

THIS IS AN IMPASSABLE OBSTACLE!

PULL, KIDS!

TUG

SNAP!

BOUNCE

YIKES!

THIS SPORTS TRIAL ISN'T VERY SPORTING NOW!

YES, VIEWERS, IT SEEMS TO HAVE BEEN A TRIAL OF TEACHER'S PATIENCE!

UNFORTUNATELY, WE CANNOT SHOW YOU THE LAST EVENT, WHICH IS THE MARATHON—THE WHACKING MARATHON!

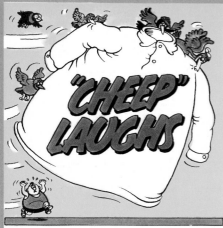

# "CHEEP" LAUGHS

THE KIDS LOOK REALLY WORRIED! I'M NOT EXACTLY HAPPY MYSELF!

NEST-BUILDING TIME, PALS! WHEN WE'VE GATHERED MATERIALS WE'LL USE SMIFFY-BIRD'S PLAN!

ALL MY OWN WORK!

NEST DESIGN by SMIFFY-BIRD

LOOK! MY BEST STRAW HAT—RUINED!

PECKED

WE MUST BE BRAVE, NOBLE ONE!

REMEMBER—THE BIRDS MUST HAVE PEACE AND QUIET, OR THEY'LL NEST ELSEWHERE—AND THE SCHOOL WILL FALL DOWN!

SPY

FALL DOWN, EH?

EEK! STOP THAT DIN!

SSSH! DON'T SHOUT, TEACHER!

'BYE-'BYE, SCHOOL!

BOUNCE AS MUCH AS YOU LIKE— YOU WON'T MAKE ANY NOISE!

THEY'VE BURST THE PILLOWS! STOP THIS AT ONCE! STOP, I SAY!

NOW, THROUGH THE WINDOW!

WE'RE OUT—NOW TO FIX THOSE BIRDS!

Later—

THAT'S AN ODD-LOOKING NEST THEY'RE MAKING!

EDITOR'S VOICE

WELL, IT WAS DESIGNED BY SMIFFY-BIRD!

SCHOOL

THIS YEAR'S NEST-DESIGNER WILL NOW OFFICIALLY OPEN THE NEST!

THREE CHEEPS FOR SMIFFY-BIRD! CHEEP! CHEEP! CHEEP!

SLITHE

SNI

RUMBLE

WAA!
MMM! DELICIOUS!

NOT TO WORRY. HERE'S A LITTLE JELLY.

Suddenly
COW ON THE ROAD! HOLD TIGHT, KIDS!
SQUEAL OF BRAKES

NOW TO GET STUCK INTO MY GRUB. NO MORE BUMPY BUSES TO BOTHER ABOUT.
PICNIC AREA

COME TO FATTY! SLOBBER!

But
WHOOSH!
OH, NO! FOILED AGAIN!
THIS LOOKS GOOD!

CH! AN EGG! AT LEAST IF I BOIL IT I'LL GET A BITE.

No need
HO! HO! HE GOT A BITE RIGHT AWAY!
WAA!
BITE

Fatty begs for food
CAN I . . . ? ON SECOND THOUGHTS I DON'T MUCH FANCY THAT!
MUNCH!
PLEASE GIVE ME SOME OF YOUR . . . OF YOUR WHATEVER-IT-IS!
MUMBLE-MUNCH!

MAL FRIENDS? GRR! EY SCOFFED MY GRUB!

UPSET STOMACH, FAT ONE?
NO, IT'S EMPTY!
RUMBLE!
RUMBLE!

A LIKELY STORY! I KNOW HOW MUCH YOU EAT! TAKE THIS— IT'LL SETTLE YOUR STOMACH!
CASTOR OIL
BUT I'VE HAD NOTHING! HELP!

# WHEN I GROW UP

*I'D LIKE TO BE PRIME MINISTER OF THESE ISLES . . .*

# THROUGH CATS EYES

1. Meow there! Winston the Janitor's cat here — and lucky to be so with those little monsters, The Bash Street Kids, to put up with for all these years. Really, that lot are so wild David Attenborough and David Bellamy come round regularly to do programmes about them.

2. Well do I remember when the little horrors first arrived at Bash Street School, Teacher had a full head of hair then — it was those dreadful children who made him tear it out in anguish. He got no sympathy from the Kids, though — they used his hair to make false moustaches and things.

3. On that first day, I was just about to tuck into a lovely bowl of cream when they struck. The fat one came first and seconds later my bowl of cream was a bowl of nothing.

4. I'd just helped myself to some more cream when the ugly Kid appeared and curdled the lot. Even then Plug had a face that made a warthog look like Miss World.

5. Danny, the leader, crashed through the wall next, bringing with him his pet mouse. Being official mouse chaser of Bash Street I leapt upon the nasty rodent. Then POW! I might have known tough Danny would have a mouse with a right hook which would put Mike Tyson to shame. From then on, it was that mouse who chased me. That was bad enough, but the pesky thing kept setting traps for me.

6. But worse was to com — after 'Erbert, the shor sighted lad, had blundere into me and flattened m perfectly formed tail, an Danny had relieved me several of my whiskers string his electric guita along came Smiffy, the bo with a lower intelligenc than a pound of mince.

He thought I was th teacher and proceeded quote his version of the tw times table for me — "Tw times one is a sausage, tw times two is Wednesda two times three is Richar two times four is the capit of Mongolia . . ."

By the time he'd eate my cat food and poure tomato sauce on me, I knev things were not going to b pleasant around Bas Street School from that da on.

8. Over the years those terrors have done some fiendish things to me, like when they gave me a trick plastic fish which I chewed for twenty-seven hours. Then there was the day they released clockwork mice stuffed with curry powder, which I pounced on . . . did you know a cat can hold seventeen bucketfuls of cold water?

11. I decided to leave Bas Street School after that get an easier jo Unfortunately, the Jo Centre wasn't looking f Moggy Lion Tamers Crocodile Wrestlers.

10. I thought they were being nice to me once when I was presented with a bag of sweets by Smiffy. Sadly the idiot had chosen aniseed balls, which, as you know, attract dogs. You might be interested to know I can run faster than Ben Johnson with two hundred snarling mutts in pursuit.

**7.** Along came Toots next. "Thank goodness!" I thought. "A sweet, little girlie!" Sweet? I've seen sweeter lemons! This evil minx had an unusual line in perfume — she made her own with liquid manure, onions, old socks, rancid cheese and rotten eggs. this Eau de Sewer, as she called it, she kindly let me sample with the aid of her water-pistol. I was having soapy baths for weeks after and even then a skunk keeled over when I passed its cage at the local zoo, such were the fumes from my fur.

· That lazy Janitor master f mine doesn't help. He eaves me to do all the weeping up, which is a hammoth task with the mount of rubbish the Kids eave lying around. One day d swept up a veritable verest of trash and the ids decided they would ee who could be first to each the summit . . . a ndslide ensued with you now who underneath. fter I'd managed to dig my vay out, it took me days to ut away all the sticky offee papers attached to ny fur — I ended up balder han a billiard ball.

TOPPLE

**12.** My next plan was to run away, but that proved difficult as Wilfrid had decided to practise his knot tying using my tail instead of string. Unfortunately he'd tied it to the back bumper of Teacher's car . . . ever tried running backwards at thirty miles per hour for two miles? Still, on the bright side, Wilfrid did get his knot tying badge at the cubs.

**13.** I'm sure you're all wondering how I've managed to survive the reign of terror of "The Bash Street Kids" for all these years. I'll let you into a little secret — nowadays the Kids and I are the best of friends. Want to know why?

**14.** We came to a little agreement, the Kids and I. My cat pals and I love a little sing-song of an evening, so every Sunday night our Cats' Chorus gathers outside Teacher's house and belts out a selection of our favourite wails which tends to give Teacher many sleepless hours. This means the Kids get things nice and easy on a Monday morning as Teacher catches up with lost beauty sleep.

**15.** And what do I get out of it? Well, apart from a quiet life, all the kippers a cat could desire. You could say Teacher gets some kip and I get some kippers!
'Bye for meow!
Winston.

The "MOWER" the MERRIER

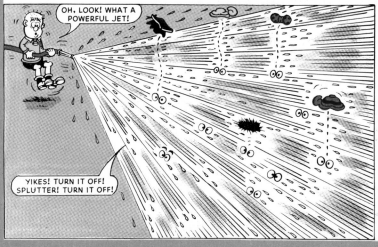

MUTTER! NOT ANOTHER . . .GROAN! . . . SCHOOL TRIP?

NO, YOU CAN ALL COME HOME WITH ME—AND TIDY UP MY GARDEN! MY AUNTY IS COMING TODAY.

GASP!

ERK! THAT'S WORSE THAN SCHOOL WORK!

HERE WE ARE—IT JUST NEEDS A LITTLE TRIM. GET THE TOOLS OUT OF THE SHED. THE SHED? OH, YES—IT'S OVER THERE SOMEWHERE!

IT'S A WILDERNESS!

HOPE THERE ARE NO LIONS ABOUT!

HERE I GO!

ERK! HOW DO YOU STEER THIS THING?

QUICK! TAKE COVER IN THE SHED!

CRASH! COLLAPSE CRUMP!

AH! I SEE THEY'VE STARTED BY DEMOLISHING THE SHED!

FOOLISH BOY! NOW, WHERE HAS PLUG GOT TO?

LIKE IT, TEACHER? GUESS WHO?

AARGH! IT'S HORRIFIC! DEMOLISH IT AT ONCE!

I'LL WATER THE LAWN— IT'S A BIT DRY.

FIRE HOSE (HIGH-POWER)

FINISHED? SPLENDID! AUNTY WILL BE HERE AT ANY MOMENT!

HEAD'S PARLOUR

ER . . . SHALL I SEND A . . . A BOAT TO MEET HER, NOBLE ONE? THE GARDEN IS RATHER W . . . WET!

VERY QUAINT, NEPHEW, DEAR! I THOUGHT YOU HAD A GARDEN—NOT A MOAT!

ANYONE KNOW A GOOD SEA SHANTY?

# WATCH THE BIRDIE

I DO ENJOY A BIT OF BIRD-WATCHING DURING THE SCHOOL HOLIDAYS.

EEK! IT CAN'T BE! IT MUSTN'T BE!

READER'S VOICE

HAS TEACHER SPOTTE A RARE SPECIES?

GOODNESS! YOU'RE RIGHT! IT IS ONE!

YOU HAVE REMARKABLE EYE-SIGHT TO BE ABLE TO SEE THAT!

OH, I DIDN'T SEE IT—

—PLUG HEARD IT WHISTLING IN AN AMERICAN ACCENT!

MY EARS ARE LIKE RADAR!

THAT MEANS IT'S FLOWN 321 MILES, 10 YARDS, 2 FEET 6 INCHES, TO GET HERE!

GOODNESS! THAT COULD BE RIGHT! AND TO THINK THAT YOU GOT "O" OUT OF 100 FOR GEOGRAPHY!

MUDPUDDLE-ON-SEA
321 MILES, 10 YDS, 2 FT., 6 INS.

GO AND PLAY ELSEWHERE!

YOU CAN'T ORDER US AROUND ON HOLIDAYS!

BIRD-SPOTTING! THAT'S WHAT WE'RE HERE FOR!

IT SAYS HERE THAT SWANS HISS WHEN THEY'RE ANGRY!

I'LL BE HISSING IN A MINUTE!

WIPE

I SAY, WHAT LUCK! I DO BELIEVE IT'S THE RARE HALF-HOODED CROW!

ERBERT'S DAD

REALLY?

# WHEN I GROW UP

*I'D LIKE TO BE A TESTER OF FINE FOOD . . .*

TOP
CLASS
ASS

THE EQUATOR IS AN IMAGINARY LINE RUNNING ROUND THE CENTRE OF THE EARTH...

HE MUST BE VERY TIRED BY THIS TIME THEN.

SIGH! WHO MUST BE VERY TIRED, UNEDUCATED URCHIN?

THE MENAGERIE LION, OF COURSE!

HAW-HAW!

Mid-morning break—

WHISPER!..YES, THAT'S WHAT WE'LL DO!

BET THAT LION SNEAKS A LIFT OR TWO.

HEAD'S RHUBARB PATCH

ZOO

DON'T WORRY, MISTER KEEPER—WE'LL BRING THEM BACK SAFE AND SOUND. HONEST! NO MONKEYING AROUND—AHEM!

Back in class—

GOOD—TEACHER'S DROPPED OFF!

BILLY WHIZZ COULD TAKE OVER WHEN THE LION GETS BLISTERS.

ZZZZ!

Lunch-break—

I THINK WE'RE FIGHTING A LOSING BATTLE TRYING TO GET TEACHER TO EAT HIS HAT.

PROFESSOR BRAIN—TEACHER EXTRAORDINARY

SPECIAL OFFER TODAY 2p OFF

CAN TURN A FOOL INTO A GENIUS IN MINUTES

HELLO! LOOK AT THIS!

GET TO WORK ON THAT BOY, PROF. HERE'S ALL OUR POCKET-MONEY.

Later—

WHAT A NICE MAN—GAVE ME A BONE FOR MY CAT!

WH-WHAT?

SPECIAL OFFER TODAY 2p OFF

I'M STUDYING A CENTIPEDE—IT HAS 184 FEET AND...

PHEW! 184 FEET! IF THAT MENAGERIE LION HAD 184 FEET HE'D MANAGE THE TRIP OK!

WHAT THE MAN SEES

And—

SCHOOL

GOSH! AMAZING! 184 FEET...

In class—

CAN ANYONE TELL ME THE HEIGHT OF NELSON'S COLUMN IN TRAFALGAR SQUARE?

GULP! EVEN I DON'T KNOW THAT ONE...SOB!

ER—EM

NEVER HAVE I COME ACROSS SUCH A —TLESS WAIF...RANT!..IF YOU EVER GET —O THE TOP OF THE CLASS I'LL EAT MY HAT!

THAT WE'D LOVE TO SEE! LET'S FIX IT SO SMIFFY GETS TO THE TOP OF THE CLASS!

RIGHT!

So—

HMM! THAT MENAGERIE LION MUST BE EVEN DAFTER THAN ME!

SMIFFY'S TOP OF THE CLASS NOW—HE'S THE ONLY ONE IN IT!

But—

BACK TO THE CLASS, LITTLE ONES—THAT WON'T WORK!

TAKE YOUR SEATS, —ER—KIDS!

OO-OO!

I'LL BORROW TEACHER'S SPECS!

Presently—

HARUMPH! WHERE ARE MY SPECS? MUST HAVE MISLAID THEM. NO MATTER—I DIMLY SEE YOU PUPILS ARE READY TO ABSORB MORE LEARNING—EXCEPT SMIFFY, OF COURSE!

SNIGGER! SMIFFY'S BOUND TO BE TOP OF A CLASS OF MONKEYS!

But—

I WAS WRONG—THE MONKEYS GOT NOTHING OUT OF A HUNDRED FOR SUMS—SMIFFY DIDN'T EVEN GET NOTHING!

ZOO

A SESSION WITH SMIFFY HAS MADE THE PROF AS DAFT AS HE IS!

GIBBER!

HUH! WE'LL NEVER GET HIM TO THE TOP OF THE CLASS—NEVER!

SILLY MAN! HE DOESN'T NEED A MAGNIFYING GLASS TO SEE THAT WALL! HOW DAFT SOME PEOPLE ARE!

HMM!

...184 FEET!

CORRECT!

AARGH! SMIFFY...IT CAN'T BE... IT IS! GO TO THE TOP OF THE CLASS!

I'VE DONE SOMETHING RIGHT ...WHATEVER IT IS!

TEA BREAK, TEACHER— HAVE A NICE HAT TO MUNCH!

ANGE! NOBODY THERE!

CLASS II B

KNOCK! KNOCK!

EH?

DON'T TELL ME—YOU'RE SMIFFY'S PARENTS!

HOW EVER DID YOU GUESS?

VERY DAFT PUPIL

SON IS UNDOUBTEDLY THE BRIGHTEST IT HAS BEEN MY PLEASURE TO TEACH!

CUTHBERT CRINGEWORTHY'S PROUD PARENTS

Meanwhile

THIS IS WHERE THE PAINTING GEAR IS KEPT.

PAINT CUPBOARD

GLOOP!

SPLUDGE!

RED PAINT

BLUE PAINT

YELLOW PAINT

PAINT CUPBOARD

OOPS!

INK

D WHAT DO YOU DO FOR A VING, MISTER PLUGSLEY?

, I'M A MALE MODEL!

ACTUALLY, HE'S A MODEL IN A HORROR MASK FACTORY!

SWOON

OUR HERO!

I'D LIKE TO SEE MY LAD, 'ERBERT, GETTING BETTER RESULTS, TEACHER!

CONCLUDES OUR OPEN HT—ERK! THE DOOR'S LOCKED!

MAY I BORROW THIS HAT-PIN, MADAM?

PULL

OPEN, YOU PESKY DOOR! OPEN!

PICK PICK

BAH! THIS MUST BE WHY IT'S CALLED AN OPEN NIGHT!

HUMPH! IMAGINE HAVING TO SPEND THE NIGHT IN SCHOOL AS WELL AS THE DAY!

WE**IGHT** *for* it

In class IIB—

WAHEY!

SEE-SAW

GREAT FUN, THIS!

Suddenly—

I'LL JOIN YOU!

ARGH! NO!

But—

OO-ER!

BOING!

And—

SPLUTTER!

GLUB!

FATTY'S CREAM SPONGE PLAY-PIECE

YOU'LL HAVE TO GO ON A DIET! NO MORE SCHOOL LUNCHES FOR YOU!

VERY WELL—I'LL JUST HAVE A SANDWICH INSTEAD.

SPLUT!

SPLURCH!

SPLAT!

GLURK! THAT FAT FOOL'S DONE IT AGAIN!

Later—

IF YOU BEAT THE BLOB STREET TUG-O'-WAR TEAM IN OUR ANNUAL CONTEST, YOU CAN HAVE THE AFTERNOON OFF.

YAHOO! WE'LL WALK IT!

VOOM!

At the contest—

HEH-HEH! EIGHT AGAINST A FAT ONE—THIS'LL BE EASY!

TAKE THE STRAIN . . .

COST US AN AFTERNOON OFF, THE GUZZLING GLUTTON!

. . . PULL!

TING-A-LING!

I KNOW THAT SOUND!

BASH STREET SCHOOL WINS!

URF!

# WHEN I GROW UP

### I'D LIKE TO BE THE FAMOUS "BEANO" ED . . .

# "WOOD" YOU BELIEVE IT?

HOW OFTEN HAVE I TOLD YOU NOT TO USE THE DOOR AS A DARTBOARD?

BUT, SIR . . .

NONE OF YOUR EXCUSES— BEND OVER!

THIS WILL HURT ME MOR THAN IT HURTS YOU.

Soon—

SHOCKING! THEY'RE SIMPLE!

WE CAN'T DO THESE SUMS!

PERHAPS—BUT WE CAN'T DO THEM BECAUSE THE WOODWORM ARE EATING OUR PENCILS!

CHOMP!

CHOMP!

CHOMP!

THE HEAD MUST HEAR OF THIS!

YAROOP! RIGHT AWAY!

CHOMP!

CHOMP!

So—

THIS WILL GET THEM!

AW, POOR LITTLE THINGS!

WOOD BLOCK

I'LL PULVERISE THE PESTS WHEN THEY COME FOR THE WOOD.

In class IIB—

WAHEY! THEY'LL SOON GOBBLE UP THE WHOLE SCHOOL.

OH, DEAR!

CHOMP!

CHOMP!

Then—

I'VE OILED MY BAT FOR THE START OF THE FOOTBALL SEASON.

VERY DIM

CASTOR OIL

IDIOT! YOU'RE MEANT TO USE LINSEED OIL!

And—

LET'S NOSH THIS WOOD—YEUCH!

MUNCH

MUN

GASP! WHAT HAPPENED?

CHOMP!

CHOMP!

IT DIDN'T HURT AT ALL!

WOODWORM!

BLOIK!

WE TRIED TO TELL YOU — THEY MADE THE HOLES IN THE DOOR.

Here's a close-up of the woodworm. Remind you of anyone?

WHAT CAN WE MUNCH NOW?

WHY? ARE YOU GOING TO WHACK YOURSELF?

SOMETHING MUST BE DONE ABOUT THE ... ARGH!

CHOMP!

... WOODWORM!

CHOMP!

YIKES! I'M INCLINED TO AGREE!

Soon—

YOU MUST SET A WOODWORM TRAP, JANITOR.

CHOMP! CHOMP! CHOMP!

I CAN HEAR THEM CHOMPING — THEY MUST BE COMING INTO MY TRAP.

OOF!

THUD!

TEE-HEE!

CHOMP!

SCRUMTIUOUS!

CHOMP!

GLUMPH!

WE'RE LEAVING! THE WOOD AROUND HERE TASTES AWFUL!

SMIFFY'S SAVED THE SCHOOL!

BAH!

MY HERO!

JUST AS WELL THE WOODWORM DIDN'T NOTICE SMIFFY'S HEAD — IT'S SOLID WOOD!

# Gifted Children

The last day before the Christmas holidays—

YOU'LL FIND A LITTLE SOMETHING FOR EACH OF YOU ON THE TREE . . .

♪ CHRISTMAS ROCK

WHERE'S M...

. . .AARGH!

GOODY! GOODY! AN EXCITING—

AWFULLY ADVANCED ALGEBRA

CUTHBERT

—NEW THRILLER!

CUTHBERT

SNIFF

NOT VERY BRIGHT

WHAT'S THIS? I CAN'T READ WHAT IT SAYS!

MASTERBRAIN PUZZLE GAME

YUMMY! MY FAVOURITE!

I DIDN'T KNOW YOU LIKED READING!

EDITOR'S VOICE

IT'S A CHOCOLATE BOOK! SLURP!

CHOMP!

FANTASTIC! NEW GLASSES!

I THOUGHT YOU ME... NEW "SPECTACLE... HEE! HEE!

AN EASTER EGG?

LOOK INSIDE!

WHY, CHILDREN, IT'S . . . IT'S BEAUTIFUL!

NOT HIM, SILLY READER!